INDIGENOUS AMERICAN CULTURES

Celebrating the IROQUOIS Tribes

ANNE ACCARDI

Mitchell Lane
PUBLISHERS

Parent and Caregiver Tips for Creating Nonfiction Readers

The high-interest topics in the ***Indigenous American Cultures*** series are sure to get your young reader excited about reading nonfiction. While exploring a fascinating subject, your reader will be introduced to new facts, ideas, and vocabulary.

Tips for Reading Nonfiction

Talk about Nonfiction

Explain that nonfiction books provide facts about real-world topics. When readers read nonfiction, they gain a rich understanding of the world. They build background knowledge that provides a foundation for learning and academic success.

Look at the Parts

This book contains the following helpful features. Share the purpose of each feature with your reader.

Photos, Captions, and Graphic Aids
The photos, captions, maps, diagrams, time lines, and other graphic aids in nonfiction texts contain a wealth of information. Help your reader identify different ways information can be displayed.

Sidebars
These extra tidbits of information help satisfy readers' curiosity and expand their knowledge.

Table of Contents
Located at the front of the book, this list shows the big ideas within the text and the page numbers where they can be found.

Glossary
Located at the back of the book, the glossary defines key words and phrases that are related to the topic. These words and phrases can be found in the text in colored type.

Comprehension Questions (Fact Check)
Multiple-choice questions help readers self-check to make sure they understand what they read.

Index
Located at the back of the book, the index is an alphabetical list of topics and the page numbers where they can be found.

With a little help and guidance, your reader will be on their way to enjoying and learning from nonfiction books.

Mitchell Lane
PUBLISHERS

mitchelllanepub.com

2001 SW 31st Avenue
Hallandale, FL 33009

First Edition, 2026.
Author: Anne Accardi
Designer: Rhea Magaro
Editor: Kim Thompson

Series: Indigenous American Cultures
Title: Celebrating the Iroquois Tribes / by Anne Accardi

Hallandale, FL : Mitchell Lane Publishers, [2026]

Library bound ISBN: 979-8-89260-554-0
Paperback ISBN: 979-8-89260-590-8
eBook ISBN: 979-8-89260-559-5

PHOTO CREDITS
Alamy: Maxim Ermolenko, cover, 1; Classic Image, 4; Science History Image, 5; Lebrecht Music & Arts, 6; De Luan, 8; Vespasian, 11; Philip Scalia, 12, 13; Giordanno Brumas, 14; Alex Hamer, 17; Science History Images, 18; ZUMA Press, Inc, 19; Album, 20; Marilyn Angel Wynn, 23; Vespasian, 25; North Wind Picture Archives, 28; Vespasian, 29; Public Domain: Wiki, 4, 7, 15, 21, 26, 27, 28; Shutterstock: meunierd, cover, 1; Zack Frank, cover, 1; Alina Reynbakh, 9, 10, 24; FOTOGRIN, 11; Chris Allan, 21; MarBom, 23; Wirestock Creators, 25;

CONTENTS

AN IROQUOIS CONNECTION

You probably know about the United States Constitution. It explains how the American government is set up. It tells what rights U.S. citizens have. What you may not know is that this important document was influenced by a much older system of laws.

The Iroquois **Confederacy** is a group of **Indigenous** American tribes. Its government was formed over 800 years ago. The way it works is explained in the Iroquois Law of Peace. Early American leaders knew about this law. They used it to help shape the government of the United States.

The Great Law of Peace united five tribes. It was designed to bring peace, health, and justice.

Culture Close-Up

The Iroquois Confederacy is considered to be one of the oldest **democracies** in the world.

IROQUOIS HISTORY

Nearly a thousand years ago, five tribes lived on land that is now the state of New York. Even though they spoke similar languages, the tribes had a long history of war. A leader named Hiawatha brought them together. They created the Iroquois Confederacy. It is also called the Haudenosaunee (hoo-dee-noh-SHAW-nee) Confederacy.

Chief Hiawatha

The Great Law of Peace establishes their government. It divides the tribes into smaller groups called **clans**. The oldest woman in each clan is the clan mother. It is her job to pick the clan chief. The chiefs work together to lead the Confederacy.

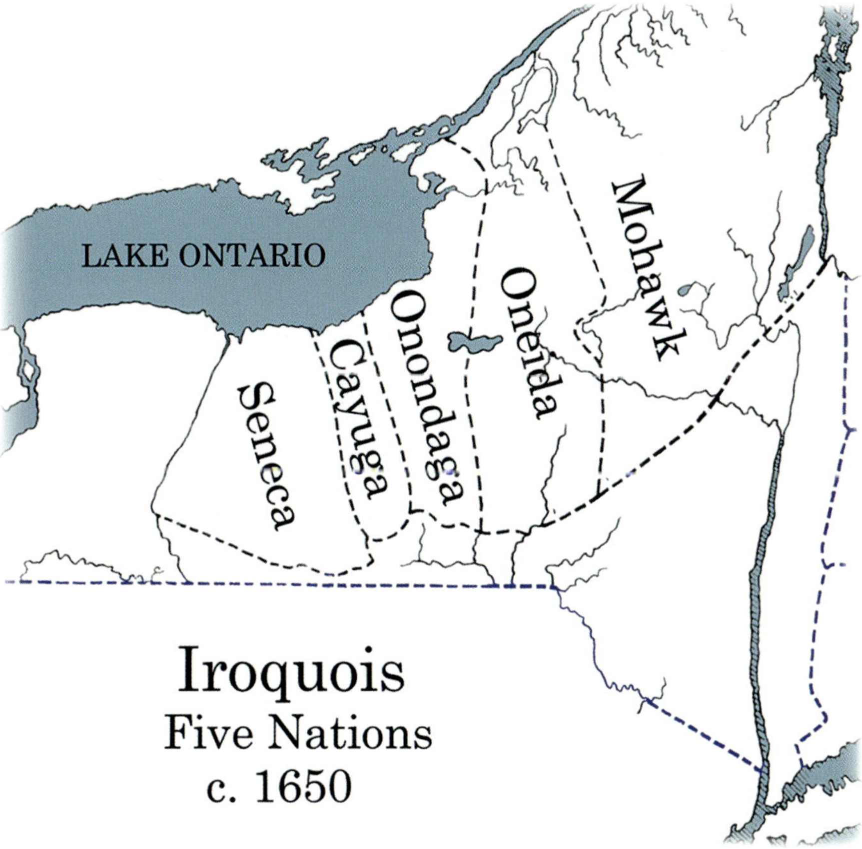

Culture Close-Up

The five tribes that formed the Iroquois Confederacy were the Cayuga, Mohawk, Oneida, Onondaga, and Seneca. The Tuscarora tribe joined in the 1700s.

When Europeans arrived in North America, the Iroquois Confederacy was strong. During the Revolutionary War, American colonies fought Great Britain to win their independence. The Iroquois sided with the British. When the British lost the war, the Iroquois lost their land. They were forced to move onto small **reservations** in the U.S. and Canada.

Today, there are about 80,000 Iroquois people in the U.S. Many live on reservations in New York and Wisconsin.

Modern Iroquois people lead ordinary modern lives. But they remember their traditional culture and find ways to keep it alive.

EXPLORING IROQUOIS PLACES

To learn more about the Iroquois, you can visit the Iroquois Museum in Howes Cave, New York. It is shaped like a traditional Iroquois **longhouse** with a long, central hallway and a door at each end.

The museum has a large collection of Iroquois art. It has exhibits about Iroquois history. At special events, you can learn skills from Iroquois artists. You can watch dances by Indigenous groups.

Traditional Iroquois longhouses were made from wood and bark. They could be 300 feet (90 meters) long.

Culture Close-Up

The museum has a children's area with a turtle pond. Kids can learn the Iroquois creation story, which says that Earth was built on the back of a giant turtle.

The Seneca are one Iroquois tribe. You can learn about them by visiting the Ganondagan (gah-NUN-dah-gan) State Historic Site in Victor, New York. More than 350 years ago, a Seneca town stood here.

Once, the town of Ganondagan had 150 buildings and 4,500 people. Its name means "town of peace."

You can tour a full-sized longhouse. It is furnished with items that show how a large Seneca family would have lived long ago.

Culture Close-Up

The Iroquois call themselves *Haudenosaunee*. The name means "people of the longhouse."

IROQUOIS LANGUAGES

Iroquois languages are part of a family of North American Indigenous languages that were once spoken throughout the Great Lakes region and beyond. Words and sentences in the languages are complex. One long word can hold a lot of meaning.

Many Iroquois languages are still spoken today. Elders teach them to young people. Mohawk is spoken by 3,000 people in the U.S. and Canada. The St. Regis Mohawk Reservation has two schools where students speak only Mohawk.

Signs on the reservation are in the Mohawk language.

Culture Close-Up

Practice these Mohawk words and phrases.
Shé:kon, skennenkó: ken? (Hello, how are you?)
Skennen'kó:wa ní:'i (I am well.)
Jane yónkya'ts (My name is Jane.)
Ó:nen (Goodbye.)

HONORING IROQUOIS TRADITIONS

Wampum are white and purple beads made from polished clam shells. They are strung together and worn on belts or sashes. The designs and patterns hold meaning. Traditionally, they were used to help people remember important events and **treaties**. They were also used for trade.

Iroquois artists still make wampum today. Some make reproductions of ancient patterns. The most famous design is on the Hiawatha Belt. This belt recorded the beginning of the Iroquois Confederacy. It has four white squares with a tree in the middle. Each symbol represents a tribe.

Iroquois tribes respect what wampum represents. When someone speaks while holding wampum, others know they are telling the truth.

Culture Close-Up

In 1989, the state of New York returned 12 important wampum belts, including the original Hiawatha Belt, to the Onondaga tribe.

Iroquois tribes invented the game of lacrosse. It is North America's oldest team sport. Long ago, deer hide was used to make the balls and nets.

Early lacrosse matches involved up to 1,000 players. They could last for days. Games were sometimes played to prepare for war or to settle fights.

Today, lacrosse is played all over the world. It continues to be played by Iroquois people. The Haudenosaunee Nationals is an Indigenous lacrosse organization. Its men's and women's teams compete on the world stage. They hope to play in the 2028 Olympic Games.

Culture Close-Up

The Iroquois tribes consider playing lacrosse to be a form of medicine. It promotes health, strength, courage, leadership, and fair play.

In the 1700s, Iroquois women had more rights than women in the American colonies. Iroquois children belong to their mothers' clan. Traditionally, a husband moved into the longhouse of his wife's family. Women owned the land and crops. They were included in tribal meetings.

Long before American women could vote, women in Iroquois tribes helped make decisions about land ownership, war, and other important issues.

Today, many Iroquois people still claim the clan identity they get from their mothers. Clan mothers still choose the chiefs for their tribe.

Wakerahkáhtste Louise McDonald Herne served as Bear Clan Mother for the Mohawk Nation.

Culture Close-Up

Iroquois clans are named for animals. Some clans are the Turtle Clan, Bear Clan, Wolf Clan, Deer Clan, and Beaver Clan.

IROQUOIS CELEBRATIONS

The Iroquois calendar has 13 moons, or months. There is a celebration for each moon. Moon celebrations are held to thank the natural world and the Creator. They include prayers, singing, and dancing.

Traditional Haudenosaunee Moon Ceremonies

1. Midwinter
2. Maple Syrup
3. Thunder
4. Planting
5. Strawberry
6. Green Beans
7. Green Corn
8. Harvest
9. Storing Food
10. Giving Thanks
11. Hunting
12. Long Nights/Storytelling
13. Snow Moon

In spring, Iroquois tribes hold ceremonies to give thanks for rain and planting seeds. In summer and fall, they celebrate growing and harvesting crops and hunting for meat. In winter, their celebrations involve telling stories about their hunting adventures.

A Seneca man shows native sweetgrass plants.

Culture Close-Up

The Oneida call strawberries *Awʌ́hihte̲'*, which is also their name for the month of June. They mash strawberries with corn to make bread, dry them to make fruit leather, or use their juice to make a berry drink.

Each year, the Iroquois Museum in Howes Cave, New York, hosts the Iroquois Arts Festival. Artists sell their work. There is storytelling, traditional dancing, and delicious food.

At the festival, you can learn about Iroquois history. An **archaeologist** might explain how the Iroquois made tools out of stone. A biologist might teach you about the native birds in Iroquois homelands.

FAMOUS FACES

There are many famous Iroquois people. Devery Jacobs is a Mohawk actor and filmmaker. She stars in the TV show *Reservation Dogs*. It is one of the first shows to have all Indigenous writers.

Thomas Longboat was an Onondaga distance runner. In 1907, he became the first Indigenous person to win the Boston Marathon. He competed in the Olympics for Canada in 1908. Longboat helped make marathon running an international sport.

Culture Close-Up

A Mohawk woman, Pauline Johnson, was a famous poet and performer in the 1800s.

LESSONS FROM THE IROQUOIS

Haudenosaunee people celebrate their culture and honor their **heritage**. They give thanks for the natural world and try to make decisions that will be good for future generations.

Long ago, warring tribes came together to form the Iroquois Confederacy. Their story is a powerful example of unity. All Americans can learn about peace and problem solving from one of the world's oldest democracies.

GLOSSARY

archaeologist (ahr-kee-AH-luh-jist): someone who studies human history by looking at old places and objects

clans (klanz): smaller groups of people within a tribe; groups of people descended from a common ancestor

confederacy (kuhn-FED-ur-uh-see): a union of groups that join together for a common purpose

democracies (di-MAH-kruh-sees): governments in which the people choose their leaders and help make decisions

heritage (HER-i-tij): traditions and beliefs that people consider to be an important part of their history

Indigenous (in-DI-juh-nuhs): the earliest known inhabitants of a place

longhouse (LONG-hous): a large, long house where many Indigenous families lived together

reservations (rez-ur-VAY-shuhnz): areas of land set aside by the government for ownership by an Indigenous American tribe

treaties (TREE-tees): agreements between two or more groups of people

wampum (WAH-puhm): beads that are made of polished shells, that are strung in patterns on belts or sashes, and that were used by some Indigenous Americans as forms of communication, treaty agreements, or money

FACT CHECK

1. How many moon festivals do the Iroquois celebrate?

   A. 5 B. 12 C. 13

2. In what country do Iroquois people live other than the United States?

   A. Canada B. Mexico C. England

3. What is wampum?

   A. a wooden pole B. food C. beads strung in a pattern

4. What leader helped create the Iroquois Confederacy?

   A. Mohawk B. Hiawatha C. Seneca

Answers: 1. C, 2. A, 3. C, 4. B

FURTHER READING

Bruchac, Joseph. *Peacemaker.* Dial Books, 2022.

Favor, Lesli J. *The Iroquois Constitution: A Primary Source Investigation of the Law of the Iroquois (Great American Political Documents).* Rosen, 2003.

Weso, Tom Pecore. *Native American Stories for Kids: 12 Traditional Stories from Indigenous Tribes across North America*. Callisto Kids, 2022.

ON THE INTERNET

Haudenosaunee Confederacy
www.haudenosauneeconfederacy.com
Visit the official website of the Iroquois Confederacy.

Iroquois Museum
www.iroquoismuseum.org
See online exhibits or take virtual tours to learn more about the Iroquois.

Native American Hall of Fame
nativehalloffame.org
Find biographies of well-known Indigenous Americans from the 1860s to the present.

INDEX

ABOUT THE AUTHOR

Anne Accardi is an author from Kansas City, Missouri. She is thrilled to share facts about Indigenous Americans with young people. She loves history and finding ways to connect the past with the present and future. When she's not reading or writing, you can find Anne in a library, museum, or movie theater.